Assessment for Learning in the EYFS

MARIANNE SARGENT

Published 2011 by Featherstone Education
Bloomsbury Publishing plc
50 Bedford Square, London,
www.acblack.com

ISBN 978-1-4081-4050-5

Text © Marianne Sargent
Design © Lynda Murray
Photographs © Shutterstock 2011, Fotolia 2011
Photos on pages 9,16, 34, 40, 55 and 60 with kind permission of Acorn Childcare Ltd, Milton Keynes

Printed in Great Britain by Latimer Trend & Company Ltd

This book is produced using paper that is made from wood grown in
managed, sustainable forests. It is natural, renewable and recyclable.
The logging and manufacturing processes conform to the environmental
regulations of the country of origin.

To see our full range of titles visit **www.acblack.com**

Contents

Part One
Introducing AFL (Assessment for Learning)

Part Two
Developing AfL practice in early years settings

Part One

Introducing AFL
(Assessment for Learning)

Introduction

This book draws upon experience I gained while teaching in a primary school in Jersey. The school was working in partnership with researchers from King's College, University of London to implement Assessment for Learning (AfL) practice in Key Stage 2 classrooms. Over a period of two years various techniques were developed and shared with teachers across the school and gradually introduced to all classrooms, including nursery and reception.

Aims of the book

The general focus of AfL has previously been aimed at Key Stage 2 and above. This book has been written in acknowledgement of the fact that younger children are just as capable of participating in decision-making about the teaching and learning they experience. By explaining the theory and referring to contemporary research, this book aims to demonstrate why assessment is an important formative tool to help further children's learning. It explains what AfL is, the reasoning behind it and how it can be implemented in the early years classroom.

There are practical examples throughout to help practitioners use AfL in Foundation Stage and Key Stage 1 settings. Although it is most relevant to those who work in schools, the strategies covered are equally applicable and useful to practitioners and children in any early years setting. The terms practitioner, teacher, school and setting are used throughout to reflect this.

The first part of the book takes a brief look at the purposes of assessment and explains the principles that underpin AfL practice. It also outlines relevant educational theory and research, and considers influential approaches to early years teaching and learning, in order to demonstrate how AfL practice supports effective early years pedagogy. It concludes by looking at how AfL promotes the aims and principles of the Early Years Foundation Stage (EYFS) and the National Curriculum for Key Stage 1.

The second part of the book takes a more detailed look at AfL. It is divided into four sections that each focus on one particular aspect of AfL practice:

- Creating a positive learning culture

- A talking and thinking classroom

- Planning AfL

- Assessment and feedback strategies

Each section provides explanation of the practice and consideration of the key strategies involved. Throughout there are suggestions for AfL techniques and activities aimed specifically at children from three to seven years. These are provided with the intention of enabling children in the early years to actively participate in assessment procedures.

There are also suggestions for techniques and activities that aim to prepare children and help them to develop the skills they will need in order to participate in AfL practice as they progress through their education. Techniques that are currently used in schools are outlined and explained with the intention of helping early years practitioners visualise how children in Key Stage 2 and above are being taught. This is to provide a context and help practitioners understand what the children in their care will be doing when they are older.

The purpose of assessment

Although the purpose of assessment will be obvious to many teachers, this book is intended to cater for early education students, as well as early years practitioners with a range of qualifications and experience. Therefore, it will help to start by setting the context with a brief look at the various types of assessment and considering the uses of each.

Baseline assessment

This is an initial assessment that gives an indication of a learner's current level of attainment. The results of a baseline assessment are used to plan starting points for learning and are then referred back to, in order to measure a learner's future progress.

Summative assessment

This is most commonly associated with examinations and tests that aim to determine how much has been learned at the end of a certain period. It is carried out at the conclusion of a unit of work or topic, or at the end of an academic term or year. Summative assessment is sometimes referred to as assessment 'of' learning and aims to show where a learner is at a particular point in time.

Formative assessment

This type of assessment is on-going and used to inform continuing planning and teaching. Black and Wiliam define formative assessment as when 'evidence is actually used to adapt the teaching work to meet the needs' (2001, p.2). Formative assessment is used to ascertain where learners are in their learning and to help them move forward. This might be on a minute-to-minute basis as an activity progresses, or a day-to-day or week-to-week basis as a theme or topic evolves. In the Foundation Stage this involves regular observations of the children's activities, as well as constant dialogue and discussion between practitioners and children. Formative assessment is the focus of this book.

The importance of formative assessment

'Day-to-day assessment is a natural, integral and essential part of effective learning and teaching. Teachers and children continually reflect on how learning is progressing, see where improvements can be made and identify the next steps to take.'

(DCSF, 2008c)

The Assessment Group of the British Educational Research Association, now known as the Assessment Reform Group (ARG), have been researching classroom assessment and its impact upon learning for over 20 years. The ARG works with government policy makers, local authorities, teaching organisations and teachers to help improve understanding of the purpose and impact of assessment. The group commissioned Professor Paul Black and Professor Dylan Wiliam to carry out an extensive review of the research literature concerning classroom assessment and its impact upon learning. Black and Wiliam found that, regardless of country, age group or subject area, formative assessment is the key to consistently and substantially improving learners' chances (Wiliam, 2009). In other words, they found that the effective use of formative assessment leads to successful learning.

Black and Wiliam (2001) called upon the Government to redress the balance with regard to the focus of its educational policy on assessment. They suggested that the Government's concentration on national testing resulted in a focus on summative assessment and proposed that any serious attempt at raising standards should be aimed at improving the use of formative assessment in classrooms. The ARG (1999) supported this view and set out proposals for a change in policy priorities in favour of Assessment for Learning.

Assessment for Learning (AfL)

AfL is most clearly defined by the ARG in their guidance for teachers:

> *'Assessment for Learning is the process of seeking and interpreting evidence for use by learners and their teachers to decide where the learners are in their learning, where they need to go and how best to get there.'*

(ARG, 2002)

The basic premise of AfL is that learning is more successful if the learner is given greater responsibility and awarded more control over their learning. This involves including learners in decision making about what they want and need to learn, as well as helping them to develop the skills needed to assess themselves during the learning process.

Principles of AfL

The ARG (2002) worked together with experts in educational assessment as well as educational practitioners to develop 10 Principles of Assessment for Learning. These were devised with the intention of outlining the essential features of AfL in order to help teachers better understand the aims of AfL and help them to develop AfL techniques. The principles are outlined below with a brief explanation for each:

1 **AfL is part of effective planning**

Children are involved in planning topics and projects, helping to identify areas where they lack knowledge or would like to find out more. AfL works best if planning is open and flexible. Planning ensures there is opportunity for practitioners to pause, reflect and revisit on a regular basis. Planning helps practitioners to clearly communicate learning objectives and success criteria. It also details strategies for how learners will take part in the assessment process.

2 **AfL focuses on how children learn**

AfL helps children to become aware of the process of learning. Practitioners help children to think about how they are learning as well as what they are learning.

3 **AfL is central to classroom practice**

Practitioners prompt children to demonstrate their knowledge through constant dialogue and carefully considered questioning. Throughout this process, practitioners continually assess the children's understanding and use a variety of strategies to help them move on.

4 **AfL is a key professional skill**

Practitioners understand the purpose and importance of formative assessment. They are able to use their observations to judge where children are in their learning and what they need to do to improve. Practitioners use a number of techniques to help children learn how to self-assess.

5 **AfL is sensitive and constructive**

Feedback is sensitive and constructive and is focused on the work rather than the individual. Much effort is put into developing a respectful classroom culture that encourages all children to participate without fear of failure or ridicule. All contributions are valued for their worth in terms to furthering understanding.

6 **AfL fosters motivation**

AfL aims to instil within learners a willingness to learn by emphasising achievement and highlighting progress. Children are empowered by gaining skills in self-assessment and learning how to improve their work.

7 AfL promotes understanding of goals and criteria
Learners are involved In deciding what they learn. They are also encouraged to think about what they need to do in order to achieve their goal. Practitioners devise success criteria in collaboration with children and set them out in child-friendly language. Children learn how to self and peer assess by applying success criteria to their work.

8 AfL helps learners know how to improve
Rather than allocate grades or hand out rewards, practitioners provide constructive feedback that helps children to recognise and develop their strengths.

9 AfL develops the capacity for self-assessment
Children are encouraged to take control over their own learning. They become independent learners by reflecting on their work and deciding how it can be improved.

10 AfL recognises all educational achievement
AfL recognises the achievements of all children. The use of AfL techniques aims to ensure that all children achieve their best.

Key strategies for implementing AfL

With these principles in mind, Black and Wiliam went on to devise a number of strategies for implementing AfL in the classroom. Shirley Clarke (2008) builds upon these in her own extensive research into formative assessment, and suggests seven key strategies for effective and successful formative assessment:

1 Creating a positive classroom culture where all feel that they can achieve and improve.

2 Planning topics, themes, projects or lessons within meaningful contexts and at an appropriate level, and involving pupils in the process.

3 Clarifying learning objectives and establishing pupil-generated and therefore pupil-owned success criteria.

4 Planning and facilitating effective classroom discussion and worthwhile questioning.

5 Involving pupils in analysis and discussion about what excellence consists of and how to meet success criteria.

6 Enabling pupils to be effective self and peer-evaluators.

7 Making time for review and provision of time to act on feedback from teachers and pupils.

This book considers the underlying AfL principles and related strategies with regard to early years practice.

Formative assessment as part of effective early years pedagogy

This section takes a brief look at some of the pioneering theories in education, as well as relevant research findings and ideas taken from influential approaches to early years practice. This is to demonstrate how AfL supports effective early years pedagogy.

Key educational thinkers

AfL practice seeks to empower learners by teaching them skills to be able to move their own learning forward. Educators are viewed as facilitators in this process, helping children to develop the skills they need in order to acquire knowledge for themselves. The philosophy behind this approach is represented in the theories of some of the key educational theorists as explained below.

Jean Piaget: active learning

Piaget highlighted the role of the learner in the knowledge-gathering process. Rather than being fed knowledge, he suggested that children should be allowed to discover information for themselves through their own active investigation of the world. He believed that children construct their own knowledge through their interactions with the environment around them. There are connections with the underpinning principles of AfL here. AfL practice is designed to encourage learners to be independent and actively involved in the management of their own learning.

Lev Vygotsky: the zone of proximal development

Vygotsky believed that children develop their knowledge through interaction with expert others. He described an unassisted child as learning within her zone of actual development. He explained the educator's role as helping the child to move into her zone of proximal development by offering support and assistance that helps to extend her learning further:

'…what is the zone of proximal development today will be the actual developmental level tomorrow – that is, what a child can do with assistance today she will be able to do by herself tomorrow.'

(Vygotsky, 1978, p.87)

In order for practitioners to be able to move children forward, they need to have a good idea about the aptitude, ability and current level of understanding of each individual. Formative assessment plays an essential part in this process. Practitioners join children's play, share stories and facilitate group investigation. All the while, they observe the children and engage them in thought-provoking discussion, which enables them to gain an insight into and make judgements about the children's current understandings. This enables practitioners to target questioning and support with the aim of helping the children to develop new ideas and increase their knowledge. Jerome Bruner describes this as

'scaffolding' the children's learning through joint involvement episodes featuring quality interaction between adults and children

(Wood et al, 1976).

Reuven Feuerstein: instrumental enrichment

Feuerstein developed the instrumental enrichment programme to help students develop transferable thinking skills that enable them to become independent learners. This includes learning about metacognition, or thinking about thinking. The idea is that students learn to think about their own thinking and in doing so learn how to teach themselves. AfL aims to do exactly this. Practitioners work alongside children, observing, listening, talking and questioning, while formatively assessing how they can help those children move on in their thinking and learning. Children are taught critical thinking skills that help them to learn from interacting with others, reflecting upon their ideas, adjusting their thinking and assessing their own progress. This all contributes towards helping children to become independent life-long learners.

Furthermore, Feuerstein believed that intelligence is not fixed but can be modified with assistance. He described this as mediated intervention. This is also supported by one of the principles of AfL that, if given adequate support, all children are able to progress and achieve.

Benjamin Bloom: taxonomy of critical thinking skills

Bloom devised a hierarchy of progressively more demanding critical thinking skills. According to this theory, each of the skills builds upon the other with learners increasing in cognitive ability as they become accomplished in one and move onto the next. The most basic skill is recalling knowledge and the highest order skill is reflecting upon and evaluating information:

Evaluation
Reflecting upon information to formulate opinion

↑

Synthesis
Using information to come up with creative ideas

↑

Analysis
Examining and re-organising information to help make sense

↑

Application
Applying information to a range of contexts and situations

↑

Comprehension
Understanding the meaning of information

↑

Knowledge
Recalling information

Clarke (2008) and Spendlove (2009) have used Bloom's taxonomy to formulate questions that specifically aim to develop each different type of thinking skill. AfL practice aims to move children on from being able to answer simple knowledge-based questions to those that require evaluative skills. Furthermore, children are encouraged to develop enquiring minds and begin to learn the questioning skills they need to be able to further their own learning. This is explained and illustrated later in the book.

Key early years research

Over the past decade a great deal of research has been undertaken with the aim of finding out what constitutes good practice in early years education. This research has informed the development of early educational policy and curricular documentation. The following research projects have been particularly influential and each highlights the importance of formative assessment for effective early learning:

Study of Pedagogical Effectiveness in Early Learning (SPEEL)

This study sought to identify the characteristics of effective approaches to teaching and learning in the early years. It focused upon the role of the adult and looked at the attitudes, skills, knowledge and understanding of practitioners and how these impact upon children's learning. The study found that although practitioners demonstrate an understanding of the importance of intervening and scaffolding children's learning during activities, many find this difficult because they are unsure how to do so. The study also highlights a lack of understanding in terms of the formative use of assessment to meet the needs of individual children. The report recommends practitioners 'be taught how to interact with children at the level of teaching whilst not undermining children's confidence in their own skills and abilities' (Moyles et al, 2002, p.135). AfL practice aims to do this.

Researching Effective Pedagogy in the Early Years (REPEY)

This study into the impact of staff-approaches to teaching upon the learning of young children also highlights the importance of carefully orchestrated intervention from adults. It underlines the importance of formative assessment, and in particular the use of feedback during activities for meeting the needs of individual children (Siraj-Blatchford et al, 2002). This is specifically what AfL aims to achieve.

Effective Provision of Pre-school Education Project (EPPE)

This project looked at the effects of early education on young children's development and again emphasises the importance of good quality adult-child interactions for furthering learning. The study found that the use of open questions to engage children in sustained shared thinking, together with modelling and formative feedback from adults, leads to better cognitive outcomes (Siraj-Blatchford et al, 2004).

Key approaches to teaching and learning

Each of the above research studies and theorists share the common thread in their findings that effective early learning is achieved through fostering independence in young children by helping them to develop their creative and critical thinking skills. The following educational approaches also support this philosophy:

Reggio Emilia Approach

In Reggio Emilia pre-schools in Northern Italy, children are given opportunities to engage themselves in self-directed activities that involve in depth exploration and investigation. The adults work alongside the children, questioning and encouraging them to find reasons and explanations. This constant communication and collaboration is seen as fundamentally important to the learning process:

> 'Learning does not take place by means of transmission or reproduction... it is a process of relations – a process of social construction. We thus consider knowledge to be a process of construction by the individual in relation with others, a true act of co-construction.'

(Rinaldi, 2006, p.125)

The role of the teacher is to ensure the children's ideas and theories are acknowledged and respected by creating a safe listening culture within the setting. Rinaldi (2006) explains that the communication and exchange of ideas between children is just as important. She explains that children's knowledge and understand develops and changes as a result of being exposed to each other's views and opinions. AfL practice mirrors this approach, encouraging constant dialogue and reflection that aims to help children develop skills in self and peer-assessment.

New Zealand: Te Whãriki

The Te Whãriki curriculum framework consists of five strands – well-being, belonging, contribution, communication and exploration. Each of these are viewed as essential areas of learning and development, representing a view of education as something that should holistically develop the personal, social and emotional aspects of the person, as well as their academic abilities.

The framework represents a similar philosophy to Reggio Emilia in that it places much emphasis upon the benefits of active exploration and constant communication between children and adults. The aim of the curriculum is to help children 'to grow up as confident and competent learners' and lay 'the foundations for successful future learning' (New Zealand Ministry of Education, 1996, p.9). This is reminiscent of the principles that underpin the AfL philosophy.

Critical skills practice

The critical skills programme was devised in the United States and introduced to the United Kingdom in late 1990s. The programme, highly endorsed by Professor Tedd Wragg, focuses upon teaching children the problem-solving, decision-making and collaborative skills they will need to become proficient life-long learners. It involves presenting children with real-life problems and challenges. Children are allocated roles and work together to find solutions.

Critical skills practice involves using many of the same techniques associated with AfL, such as involving children in planning activities and designing success criteria; encouraging children to work together and promoting reflection and self-assessment. References to Vicki Charlesworth's (2005) experience of developing critical skills practice with Foundation Stage children in Jersey can be found throughout this book.

The project approach

This approach involves taking an area of interest to the children and using it as the basis for in-depth research and investigation. Long-time advocates of the approach, Professor Lilian Katz and Professor Sylvia Chard (2000) explain that the aim of project work is to develop a disposition for learning by providing a meaningful context for children to gain knowledge and practise important skills. Carrying out a project is a cyclical process involving open-ended planning that is informed by on-going observation and assessment. This requires making time for constant reflection and discussion between practitioners and children (Sargent, 2011).

This is another example of a formative approach to teaching and learning that revolves around the effective use of assessment information. There are references to useful strategies taken from this approach throughout this book.

Key policy

AfL practice also supports the aims of Every Child Matters and the United Nations Convention on the Rights of the Child:

Every Child Matters

The incorporation of AfL practice into Foundation Stage teaching contributes towards meeting the Every Child Matters outcome enjoy and achieve, and in particular the aims of getting children 'ready for school' and helping them to 'achieve stretching national educational standards'. It also supports the outcome make a positive contribution, aiming to help children to 'develop self-confidence and successfully deal with significant life changes and challenges' (DfES, 2005).

United Nations Convention on the Rights of the Child

Article 12 of the Convention ensures respect for the views of the child (UNICEF, 2011). It states that adults should take the views and opinions of children into consideration when making decisions that affect them. AfL practice is all about involving children in their own learning; giving them opportunities to make choices about what they learn. It teaches them skills in self-assessment and helps them to take responsibility for their own progress.

AfL and the curriculum

Over the past decade the English, Welsh, Scottish and Northern Irish Governments have all been gradually and steadily working towards incorporating AfL practices into curriculum guidance across all ages and stages.

Scotland

The Scottish Government launched the Assessment is for Learning programme in 2002 and it was rolled out across all schools in Scotland by 2007. The Curriculum for Excellence is supported by guidance that puts assessment at the heart of teaching and learning. This includes the promotion of high quality interaction that fosters sustained shared thinking and the involvement of learners of all ages across the key stages in reflection upon their own learning.

(LTS, 2011)

Northern Ireland

The Council for the Curriculum, Examinations and Assessment in Northern Ireland linked up with the ARG in 2004 to carry out a research project that led to the widespread implementation of AfL practices across Northern Irish schools. This included the Foundation Stage, where assessment is recognised as fundamental to the learning process, and early years guidance recommends developing AfL practices through effective questioning and oral feedback.

(CCEA, 2006)

Wales

From 2005 to 2008 the Welsh Assembly Government ran a pilot programme focused upon developing thinking and assessment for learning in schools. The success of this pilot led to the programme being extended across Wales. The Foundation Phase Framework promotes the involvement of all children in their own learning by fostering active approaches to teaching and learning that encourage creative and critical thought.

(DCELLS, 2008)

England

In 2008 The Assessment for Learning Strategy was launched as part of the National Primary Strategy. The strategy aims to improve pupil progress by involving children in their own learning and making it more meaningful (DCSF, 2008a). The EYFS explains that AfL is part of everyday practice in the early years as practitioners continually observe children and use the information gathered to inform on-going planning.

(DCSF, 2008b)

Teachers' standards

AfL practice is now embedded in teaching and learning across foundation, primary and secondary education throughout the UK. AfL strategies are taught in initial teacher training programmes and the new Teachers' Standards (effective from September 2012), emphasise those aspects of teaching and learning that use formative assessment to promote pupil progress, which are all features of AfL practice.

'A teacher must:

- Promote good progress and outcomes by pupils:

  - plan teaching to build on pupils' capabilities and prior knowledge;

  - guide pupils to reflect on the progress they have made and their emerging needs;

  - encourage pupils to take a responsible and conscientious attitude to their own work and study.

- Make accurate and productive use of assessment:

  - make use of formative and summative assessment to secure pupils' progress;

  - use relevant data to monitor progress, set targets, and plan subsequent lessons;

  - give pupils regular feedback, both orally and through accurate marking and encourage pupils to respond to the feedback.'

(DfE, 2011a)

Ofsted survey

In 2007 the Office for Standards in Education (Ofsted) carried out a survey of primary and secondary schools, evaluating the impact of approaches to assessment in English and mathematics. The survey found that AfL practice was 'better developed and more effective' in the primary schools than secondary (Ofsted, 2008, p.4). It also found that the most successful schools were those that had benefited from strong support and direction from leaders, resulting in a consistent approach throughout the school. Ofsted's report points out that simply using AfL techniques is not enough: teachers need to know how to guide children to improve their work and meet targets. This involves training teachers to ensure they understand the underlying rationale of AfL practice.

This survey highlights the importance of including teachers and practitioners from all ages and stages of education in the development and implementation of AfL practice. The most successful schools are those that work to ensure that AfL is consistently implemented across the whole school. This means including early years professionals in training with the aim of introducing AfL to the youngest children.

AfL in the EYFS

The themes and commitments of the EYFS aim to improve outcomes for young children in accordance with the Every Child Matters agenda. If we take each of the four themes and consider them in relation to the principles that underpin AfL practice, you can see how it supports this aim:

A Unique Child

Children are viewed as individuals with varying needs and rates of development.
This requires a personalised approach to teaching and learning. The use of AfL strategies makes supporting individual learners more manageable by encouraging children to take an active role in the learning process by discussing and thinking about their own learning.

All children are recognised as citizens who have rights and entitlements.
This involves making time to listen, as well as working to ensure that all children are able to communicate their views and opinions. AfL strategies used with older children can be adapted for use with younger children. Young children and those with additional needs are just as capable of taking an active role in their education.

Positive Relationships

Children's attitudes to learning challenges are dependent upon positive relationships with others.
This requires a holistic approach that takes account of personal, social and emotional development as well as academic. AfL practice involves creating a safe and secure learning environment with a supportive ethos that values the contributions of all. This helps to ensure that children have a positive learning experience and that they feel motivated to learn.

Practitioners learn about each child and use this information to support and extend learning.
This involves practitioners creating regular opportunities for children to communicate their thoughts and ideas. AfL strategies have been designed in recognition of the importance of giving children straightforward methods of communicating their understandings with practitioners. Such strategies also enable practitioners to listen to large numbers of children and gain an overview of the understanding of the group as a whole.

Enabling Environments

Planning stems from the children's interests, development and needs.
This involves carrying out regular observations and using these to inform on-going planning. Observations are shared, discussed and reflected upon with other professionals and the children. This everyday Foundation Stage practice is what AfL is all about.

Learning is a continuous journey through which children build on what they know and take on new challenges.
This is supported by a personalised approach that aims to meet individual needs and extend each child's particular talents. AfL practice involves teaching children how to self-assess, recognise their strengths and pin-point those areas where they need to develop.

Learning and Development

Children have independence and control over their learning.
This involves actively involving children in making decisions about their learning. They are given opportunities to find out about those aspects of the world that interest them the most. They gain a sense of achievement from watching their understanding grow. AfL practice is all about helping children to develop the skills they need to be independent learners. Children take an active role in assessing their own understanding and planning future steps to further it.

Understanding is transformed when practitioners help children to think critically and ask questions.
This involves constant dialogue between practitioners and children. Practitioners get involved in the thinking process with children by listening to them, helping to clarify ideas and posing challenging questions. Encouraging children to think for themselves is central to AfL practice.

Recent developments with the EYFS

At the time of writing the EYFS is under review. The review by Dame Clare Tickell (2011) praises the EYFS for the positive impact it has had upon early childhood settings and improving practice. Tickell endorses the framework's existing underlying themes and commitments, however, she makes a number of suggestions for how the framework can be slimmed down and simplified. She puts forward a case for the introduction of seven new areas of development, with particular emphasis placed upon helping children to develop essential life skills that lay the foundations for future learning. The review contains a large number of recommendations concerning all areas of the EYFS. Below is a brief summary of the recommendations that are particularly relevant to the principles of AfL:

Tickell Review recommendations

- The framework should continue to support active approaches to teaching and learning that are characteristic of effective early years practice. This means fostering play and exploration that leads to creative and critical thought.

- The curriculum should strive to prepare children for future life and learning by equipping them with the language and communication skills, physical skills, and personal, social and emotional skills they will need to successfully function in a school environment.

- There should be seven areas of learning and development:

  Three 'prime' areas:
  - Personal, social and emotional development
  - Communication and language
  - Physical development.

  Four 'specific' areas:
  - Literacy
  - Mathematics
  - Understanding of the world
  - Expressive arts and design

- Assessment should continue to constitute daily observation of children's activities in order to gain an overall picture of children's embedded learning.

- Children should be involved in assessment activities because this is an important and empowering learning experience.

- The number of early learning goals should be 'simplified and slimmed-down' from 69 to 17 in order to make summative assessment more meaningful, appropriate and manageable.

- There should be a new scale to support the early learning goals that helps practitioners to determine whether children are moving towards meeting a goal (emerging), are meeting a goal (expected) or have moved beyond a goal (exceeding).

- The level descriptors for exceeding early learning goals should be more consistent with the Key Stage 1 National Curriculum to ensure smoother transition.

Government response

In response to this review the Government has published a revised draft EYFS framework for consultation (DfE, 2011b). This consultation is due to end in September 2011 and a new framework is due to come into effect in September 2012. Following is a brief look at those aspects of the draft framework that are particularly relevant to AfL:

Proposed revised EYFS framework

- The four overarching themes and guiding principles remain broadly the same but 'Enabling Environments' is to become 'Positive environments', with emphasis placed upon building children's confidence through positive experiences that are planned to meet individual needs. In addition, the 'Learning and Development' principle makes specific reference to the importance of recognising that 'children learn in different ways at different rates' (DfE, 2011b, p.4).

- The document states that there should be a focus on 'school readiness' by fostering the development of children's cognitive, behavioural, physical and emotional capabilities. This means that practitioners should primarily focus strongly on the three 'prime' areas of learning.

- The prime areas of learning focus on the following skills and capacities:

  Personal, social and emotional development

  Self-confidence and self-awareness: children develop confidence to try new activities, talk about their ideas and say when they do or do not need help.

  - Managing feelings and behaviour: children learn how to work as part of a group or class and adjust behaviour to different situations.

  - Making relationships: children learn how to show sensitivity to others' needs and feelings and develop positive relationships with others.

  Communication and language

  Listening and attention: children learn how to listen attentively and respond with relevant comments, actions and questions.

  - Understanding: children learn how to follow instructions and how to answer 'how' and 'why' questions.

  - Speaking: children learn how to speak effectively, taking account of the listener. They learn how to connect ideas and formulate explanations.

- Characteristics of effective teaching and learning are identified as:

  - Playing and exploring: children investigate, experience and 'have a go'.

  - Active learning: children enjoy achievements and keep on trying if they encounter difficulties.

  - Creating and thinking critically: children have and develop their own ideas, make links between ideas, and develop strategies for doing things.

- Formative assessment:

  - Is described as integral to the learning and development process.

  - Involves practitioners regularly observing children and reflecting upon the findings to help gain an understanding of each child's individual interests, learning style and level of achievement.

  - Involves on-going interaction between the practitioner, child, parents and other adults.

- The Early Years Foundation Stage Profile:

  - Features 17 early learning goals, accompanied by level descriptors that define how children may be working toward, meeting or exceeding expected levels (emerging, expected or exceeding).

  - Must be accompanied by a summative 'commentary' about the children's skills and abilities with regard to the key characteristics of effective learning: playing and exploring, active learning and creating and thinking critically. This is to help ease transition by providing Year 1 teachers with information about each child's stage of learning development and individual needs.

This new document upholds many of the principles underpinning AfL. There is continued support for an active approach to teaching and learning that aims to promote children's independence and foster their creative and critical thinking skills. In addition, the new prime areas of learning and development aim to help children develop life-long critical skills that lay a foundation for future learning. There are specific references to the purpose and use of formative assessment and the importance of involving children in this process through continual discussion and reflection.

The National Curriculum: Key Stage 1

The principles that underpin AfL are also reflected in some of the purposes, values and aims of the school curriculum:

- Purposes:

  - The curriculum establishes an entitlement for all pupils to a number of areas of learning and to develop knowledge, understanding, skills and attitudes necessary for their self-fulfilment and development as active and responsible citizens.

- Values:

  - Underpinning the curriculum is a belief that education enables pupils to respond positively to the opportunities and challenges of the rapidly changing world in which we live and work.

- Aims:

  - To develop enjoyment of, and commitment to learning as a means of encouraging and stimulating the best possible progress and the highest attainment for all pupils.

  - To build on pupils' strengths, interests and experiences and develop their confidence in their capacity to learn and work independently and collaboratively.

  - To give pupils the opportunity to become creative, innovative, enterprising and capable of leadership to equip them for their future lives.

  - To enable pupils to respond positively to opportunities, challenges and responsibilities.

More specifically, assessment is described to be 'at the heart of a successful curriculum' and a 'fundamental part of good teaching and learning' (QCDA, 2011). The curriculum sets out key principles that underpin effective assessment:

- The learner is at the heart of assessment: Learners should take a central role in their own assessment. Assessment should motivate learners by helping them to understand how it can be used to help them progress.

- Assessment is integral to teaching and learning: In order to create personalised learning teachers should be able to use assessment and respond to children's needs as they arise. Interaction between learners and teachers is important in this respect. Learners should be allowed to take initiative and pursue ideas for themselves.

Assessing Pupils' Progress

Between 2004 and 2010 the Government developed Assessing Pupils' Progress (APP) alongside the AfL Strategy. This guidance for primary and secondary teachers explains the importance of gathering a broad range of evidence of pupils' learning that includes observations of children's interactions, class contributions and discussions with teachers, as well as their own self-assessments. APP is intended to ensure that assessment gathers a more detailed and comprehensive view of pupils' learning that directly informs future planning, teaching and learning (QCDA, 2011).

Recent developments

At the time of writing reviews of the National Curriculum and statutory primary assessment procedures are currently underway. Lord Bew's review of Key Stage 2 testing, assessment and accountability mentions the importance of ensuring that good formative assessment arrangements are in place in primary schools. In particular Bew makes reference to the importance of AfL practice and states that it should be continued alongside statutory summative assessments. The first phase of the call for evidence for the National Curriculum review is currently in progress and the consultation period is not due to start until 2012. The new curriculum is to be phased in from September 2013.

Part Two

Developing AfL practice
in early years settings

It is important to think about developing AfL in early years settings as a long-term undertaking that will need gradual embedding into established practice. Practitioners will need to ensure that they understand the rationale behind each AfL strategy before attempting to put it into place. The children will also need time to take the various techniques on board, understand and get used to using them.

The following sections hope to make this task more manageable by tackling one aspect of AfL practice at a time. It starts by taking a look at laying the groundwork in preparation for developing AfL and moves on to introduce various strategies and techniques that can be implemented gradually and progressively thereafter.

Creating a positive learning culture

'A supportive culture of warmth and respect fosters children's confidence, motivation, independence and well-being, enabling every child to feel valued and successful.'

(Marsden, Woodbridge and Drummond, 2005, p.5)

The first step in introducing AfL is the development of a positive learning culture. The success of AfL depends upon children wanting to engage, feeling able to contribute and believing that they have the ability to succeed. This is only possible if they are helped to gain the independence and confidence they need to be capable of managing their own learning.

A safe and secure learning community

If AfL is to succeed, children need to feel emotionally secure and happy to join in. AfL practice involves children assessing their own work as well as that of others. This makes it essential to develop a culture of respect so that children are able to do this sensitively and constructively. It is important to invest time in creating a happy and secure learning community where everyone feels safe, supported and has a sense of belonging. This means investing time in helping children get to know each other so that they feel comfortable in each other's presence. It also means helping children to feel confident about speaking in front of their peers and beginning to instil a culture of respect for everyone's views and feelings.

Community building games

The following books have many suggestions for games and activities that are useful for helping children get to know each other:

- *The Little Book of Playground Games* by Simon MacDonald (A&C Black).

- *The Little Book of Parachute Play* by Clare Beswick (A&C Black).

Circle time

For good quality circle time ideas that aim to build confidence and raise self-esteem try these resources:

- *The Little Book of Circle Time* by Dawn Roper (A&C Black).

- *Circle Time for the Very Young* by Margaret Collins (Sage Publications).

- *The Circle Book* by Jenny Mosley (Positive Press).

Personal, social and emotional awareness

For ideas to help children begin to become aware of the feelings of others and start to develop empathy try these:

- *Using the Empathy Doll Approach* by Kirstine Beeley (A&C Black).

- *Exploring Emotions* by Ros Bayley and Lynn Broadbent (Lawrence Educational Publications).

Building confidence and raising motivation

AfL practice involves children and adults working together, sharing ideas and helping to extend each other's understanding. Children need to be able to work in pairs and groups, and feed back to others. For this to succeed all children need to feel confident about taking part without fear of failure or ridicule. Therefore, it is extremely important to create a positive learning culture, where children know their contributions will be valued and appreciated, and they understand that the building of knowledge is a collaborative process.

If all children are to feel able to participate they must believe that their thinking is valued, and their ideas are appreciated and useful (Harrison and Howard, 2009). Children who feel threatened by the possible negative reaction of practitioners and peers will withdraw and not contribute. Practitioners need to convey to children that all contributions are valuable, no matter whether they are correct or not. This is an important part of establishing a learning culture. Margaret Donaldson (1978) believed that when children discover they are wrong about something they are spurred on to correct their error. Making mistakes is an essential part of learning and should be used to promote a thirst for knowledge by encouraging children to want to correct their misconceptions.

Types of feedback

How a practitioner responds to children will have an effect upon the quantity and quality of their contributions. The type of feedback that children receive will impact directly upon their self-esteem and motivation to take part.

Rewards

The use of rewards can have a negative effect upon children's motivation to learn. Children are rewarded for doing well. Those children who do not do well and fail to meet certain expectations do not receive rewards. Children who consistently fail to receive a reward lose self-esteem as well as the impetus to try. Children who regularly receive rewards may avoid anything that is too challenging in case they fail and miss out on the reward (Black and Wiliam, 2001).

Furthermore, rewards result in comparison by dividing children into good or bad achievers (Harrison and Howard, 2009). Stickers, stamps and grades encourage children to compare themselves with one another. Watching other children repeatedly receive a reward or gain a high mark helps to reinforce a belief that some children are destined to be high achievers while others are not. Those children with consistently low attainment may begin to believe that they are not as capable as others and give up trying.

Praise

Ros Bayley (2007) uses the term 'praise junkies' to describe children who constantly seek affirmation from adults. Busy practitioners, who are shown any number of different creations in a day, often use throwaway comments such as 'what a fantastic model' or 'that's a pretty painting'. Children enjoy receiving such positive praise and naturally seek more. However, rather than helping children to improve on their efforts, this type of feedback encourages them to produce more of the same, or even of less quality. Jennie Lindon (2010) adds that children who constantly hear positive feedback may grow to be intolerant of criticism. She also points out that some children may recognise that a constant stream of praise is neither warranted nor genuine, which can also negatively affect their motivation to try.

The benefits of constructive feedback

'What is needed is a culture of success, backed by a belief that all can succeed.'

(Black and Wiliam, 2001, p.6)

A fundamental principle of AfL is that all learners are able to achieve. Formative assessment is about giving children constructive feedback that they will be able to act upon to improve and progress. Constructive comments focus upon what the child produces, rather than the child herself. In other words, it is not personal and does not reflect upon the child as being a success or failure. Constructive feedback gives children the means to improve, reinforcing the belief that everyone can do better and have the ability to advance if they try with support.

Furthermore, Bayley (2007) explains that the use of evaluative comments or questions encourages children to want to achieve for themselves, rather than to impress others. Feeding back in this way also has a motivational affect because children realise that they have the capacity to improve, which makes them strive toward more impressive achievements.

The use of constructive feedback is explored and exemplified later in the book when looking more closely at assessment strategies.

Developing speaking, listening and comprehension skills

Learning within a community means talking together and listening to each other. Therefore, children need opportunities to develop their speaking and listening skills so they have the confidence to voice their own opinions, as well as the concentration and attention needed to take in what others are saying.

Getting children talking

Conversation, discussion and debate are extremely important for enabling practitioners to assess children's knowledge and understanding. This is particularly true for those working with very young children who are as yet unable to record much on paper. It is by getting children to talk that practitioners are able to find out what they are thinking. This information can then be used to target support and develop the children's understanding further. Creating a talking classroom involves getting the children to talk about everything and anything throughout the day.

There are plenty of ways that Foundation Stage and Key Stage 1 practitioners can get children talking. Some ideas are:

- Check in on arrival: Bring the children together each day in small groups to say hello, briefly share how they are feeling and tell any important news they might have.

- Discuss problems: Take time to talk about any problems that arise on a day-to-day basis. In the early years, problems will probably be related to housekeeping and resources, for example: water on the toilet floors, milk spilled on the snack table, construction bricks tipped everywhere or not enough dolls for everyone to have one each. Call a meeting, share the problem and ask for ideas about how to solve it.

- Chat over snack: Join children at the snack table and introduce a line of conversation. Ask the children to talk about what they have been doing and playing with. Ask them for their opinion about something, for example, the choice of art materials currently available or the organisation of the outdoor space. Ask them about recent events, a festival celebration or birthday party, for instance.

- Daily summary: Bring the children together at the end of the day to talk about what they have been doing and share any creations they might have produced.

More ideas

The following books have some good ideas for games and activities that help to develop speaking, listening and comprehension skills in young children:

- *The Early Years Communication Handbook* by Janet Cooper (Practical Pre-School Books).

- *The Little Book of Listening* by Clare Beswick (A&C Black).

Promoting independence

'Children learn best when they are given appropriate responsibility, allowed to experiment, make errors, decisions and choices and are respected as autonomous learners.'

(Bruce, 2005, p.41)

AfL is all about encouraging children to take charge of their own learning: to become independent learners who are able to assess their own progress and find ways to improve. This involves working to ensure that young children are involved in all aspects of the planning and delivery of the education they experience. At the most basic level this means giving children access to information about daily planning and arrangements. They should be made aware of routines in order to enable them to anticipate what lies ahead. Being armed with such knowledge helps children to be independent, organise their time and plan their play and activities. The following strategies aim to help keep children informed about and involved in the daily routine:

- Visual timetable: Take photographs of children carrying out various activities throughout the day, such as registration, snack and story time. Put together a pictorial timetable of events for each day of the week and display it at a low level for the children to check throughout each day. Children often like to visit this to see what might be coming next. This helps them to develop a sense of time, which they learn how to manage, enabling them to organise and plan.

- Plan of the day: At the start of each day ask the children if they can remember what happens on that particular day of the week. Write down the events in a list on a whiteboard and add in anything extra that might be happening. Throughout the day, revisit the list and tick them off. Make changes where needed as the day progresses. This will help the children gain a sense of the time and keep track of where they are in the day.

- Five minute countdown: Use a sand timer or a digital stopwatch with an alarm to give the children five minutes notice at the end of each session or activity. This will enable them to finish what they are doing or put things safely to one side without feeling rushed or interrupted. There is an ideal opportunity here to get children involved by allowing them to take responsibility for starting and watching the timer, and showing it around.

Furthermore, children who have been learning in an environment that encourages independence and autonomous thought will be much better equipped to learn and use AfL strategies as they progress through their education. The early years learning environment can be designed and resourced in such a way that helps children to be independent and manage their own learning. For example:

- Taking responsibility: Involving children in the management and organisation of the setting helps them to develop a sense of responsibility. Some ways of doing this are: self-registration by posting a name card in a box on the way into the setting and when having a snack; and taking charge of various areas in the setting by keeping them clean and tidy.

- Open access to resources: This allows children to make decisions about what they would like to do, and makes it possible for them to adapt plans and develop ideas without the need for adult help.

- Pictorial instructions: These help children to use various pieces of equipment independently. Examples of this include step-by-step guides to using the listening centre or computers, and photographs of children preparing a snack.

> ## More ideas
>
> There are many ways that practitioners can promote independence and autonomy in young children. For a wealth of ideas try these books:
>
> - *The Independent Learning in the Foundation Stage* by Sally Featherstone and Ros Bayley (Featherstone Education).
>
> - *Critical Skills in the Early Years* by Vicki Charlesworth, (Network Continuum Education).

A talking and thinking classroom

'Discussion is not enough: the teacher has to encourage and to listen carefully to a range of responses… and then help children talk through inconsistencies and to respond to challenges… students must be active in the process – learning has to be done by them, it cannot be done for them. The children have to close the gap between what they don't know and what they want to know and they need to be taught the skills to "close the gap"'.

(Harrison and Howard, 2009, p.6)

This section considers the importance of creating a talking and thinking classroom that facilitates AfL practice. The practitioner promotes conversation to find out where the children's current understanding lies and then helps them to further this understanding through the use of questioning to prompt further discussion. Children are taught how to listen to each other and be confident to share their emerging ideas.

AfL practice involves evaluating each other's views and ideas, offering counter-arguments and clarifying points. Black and Wiliam describe this as creating a 'culture of questioning and deep thinking in which pupils will learn from shared discussion with teachers and from one another' (2001, p.9). Being able to participate in this enables individual children to see where their own understanding is in relation to others, which is important for being able to self-assess and manage their own learning.

Effective questioning

Truly effective questioning is difficult to achieve. Using too many closed questions that require a specific answer or simple yes or no response, limit thought processes because they rarely demand that children deliberate or work anything out. This type of question is more frequently used because it needs less thought and easily runs off the tongue. Teachers often fire closed questions at children in quick succession with the aim of bringing them around to a specific answer. Unfortunately closed questions only enable practitioners to ascertain a limited amount of information about what children understand and know. Open questions are more challenging to answer and are useful for practitioners because they help gather information about the children's thought processes. Formulating this type of question requires more effort because it is more complex and requires extra thought.

Rather than regarding one type of question as better than the other, it is helpful to consider how they can be combined and used together for maximum effect. Spendlove (2009) explains that good questioning involves a balance of: closed questions that check children's knowledge of the facts and open questions that allow practitioners to ascertain how much children understand, and assist in helping to develop children's thinking further.

When formulating questions it is useful for practitioners to consider what they are trying to help children achieve. Questions are designed to make children think. There are different types of thinking and questions can be devised to develop various thinking skills. Clarke (2008) and Spendlove (2009) use Bloom's hierarchy of learning to formulate and classify kinds of question according to lower and higher order thinking. They provide examples of questions that become increasingly challenging as the skills become more sophisticated. The examples they provide are more suited to older children and so the following table provides some examples aimed at younger children:

Type of thinking skill	Question examples	
Knowledge Recalling information: describing, labelling, naming	What is this? What is happening? Where is this from?	Who is that? How do you know? How did you make that?
Comprehension Understanding the meaning of information: describing, explaining	Can you tell me what happened? Why do you think that happened? What do you think that means?	Can you tell me how that works? How do you think she feels? Can you tell me why?
Application Applying information to a range of contexts and situations: using, trying, relating, demonstrating how, predicting	Have you seen that happen before? What do you think will happen next?	What would happen if…? Can you show me how that works? What might be the best way to…? Have you tried…?
Analysis Examining and re-organising information to help make sense: analysing, questioning, testing, categorising	Can you sort these into…? What do you think this is for? What is the difference between… and…?	How can you find out if it works? Does it still work if you…? Which is the most important?
Synthesis Using information to come up with creative ideas: creating, designing, composing, revising, modifying	Can you make up your own…? Do you have any ideas about how to make…? Is there anything you want to change?	How can we make this better? Can you think of another way to do that? How can we solve this problem?
Evaluation Reflecting upon information to formulate opinion: evaluating, assessing, judging, justifying, comparing	Who agrees with…? What do you think about…? Which one do you think will work best?	Why do you think that? What might you do next time? Can you tell me why you think… is better than…?

Lower order thinking skills

Higher order thinking skills

Tips for starting, developing and sustaining a productive line of questioning:

- Start by asking closed or simple open questions that focus the children and help to lead them into more in-depth discussion. This is particularly important when working with very young children, those with additional needs or who speak English as an additional language.

- At the beginning, target lower order thinking skills, such as knowledge and comprehension, to establish how much the children know and understand already. This is important because it enables practitioners to build on the children's current understanding and extend it further.

- Take care not to ask too many questions too quickly. Give children time to think about their response. Potter (2008) suggests that pausing during conversation helps practitioners to resist the temptation to ask another question. She explains that using pauses puts the conversation into the control of the child and helps them to take the lead instead of the adult.

- It seems obvious but listen to the child and respond appropriately. The temptation is to respond with another question, which can result in a missed opportunity to extend a particular train of thought further. Instead respond with a comment on what the child has said before pausing to see if they add more.

- When a child is considering a higher order question that is more difficult to answer, help them by summarising their points and clarifying their ideas. Useful phrases and questions include, 'So what you're saying is…' 'Ok. So far you've told me…' 'Do you mean…?' 'Are you saying that…?'

- If interjecting during a child-initiated activity, begin by observing to gain a better understanding of what the children are doing. While observing think about and plan some good quality questions that will challenge the children.

- Call (2005) suggests letting children know that they are about to be asked a question so that they can prepare to answer. For example, 'That looks interesting. I would really like to know more about what you are doing. Perhaps I can ask you about that when you are finished?'

More information

The following books contain a wealth of information and advice about effective questioning:

- *Formative Assessment in Action* by Shirley Clarke (Hodder Murray).

- *Putting Assessment for Learning into Practice* by David Spendlove (Continuum).

- *The Thinking Child and The Thinking Child Resource Book* by Nicola Call (Continuum).

Getting children to respond

As well as using good quality questioning, it is important to ensure that as many children as possible have an opportunity to answer. This means finding ways that encourage those who are less confident to participate. Children will also need to be taught the skills they require in order to respond. This is especially true when working with very young children who, at the most basic level, will need help focusing and offering a relevant answer. In order to form a response a child needs to be able to: listen to the question; comprehend what is being asked; consider their answer and articulate it. Practitioners, therefore, need to teach children strategies that will enable them to formulate a considered response. The following AfL techniques are designed to help children with this.

Thinking or wait time

'One common problem is that teachers do not allow enough quiet time so that pupils can think out and offer an answer.'

(Black and Wiliam, 2001, p.8)

Research has shown that on average teachers leave just one or two seconds before providing an answer for an unanswered question (Clarke, 2005). Fast-paced questioning that gives little time for children to think of a response is less effective for a number of reasons. First, it is more likely that the same children will offer a response each time, and practitioners will tend to gravitate towards these children because their quick responses help to maintain a good teaching pace. This has a demotivating affect upon less-confident learners who need longer to think. These learners will see the same children being picked over and over again and eventually give up even thinking of an answer, let alone putting their hand up in the first place.

Providing less time to think also results in children providing a less detailed answer, with less potential for extending thinking. If all children are given a chance to think about their answer it is more likely that there will be a greater response.

Thinking time or wait time can be introduced to young children with the use of a visual cue. After asking a question the practitioner might hold up a picture of a sand timer for ten seconds while the children think. An actual sand timer is particularly effective because it helps children to understand the concept of time passing and they can see how long they have to think. A digital timer with alarm is also useful because it enables the practitioner to set different times according to the complexity of the question. In her research Clarke (2005) found that thinking time is more productive if the children are involved in something, for instance, recording their answers on a whiteboard or sharing their thoughts with a partner (these strategies are considered later on).

No hands up

In most settings, it is usually the case that children are asked to put their hand up and wait to be picked before speaking. Using this strategy teaches children about turn taking and self-control. However, as already explained, it is very likely that a pattern soon emerges where the same children quickly put their hands up each time a question is asked. Other children in the group see these same children being picked over and over to answer the questions and eventually view it as inevitable. These children begin to believe that they are not as clever as the quick responders and so withdraw. In addition, when it is the case that a large number of children put their hands up to answer a question, the few that are not yet ready to answer can be put off by the hands up all around them. To tackle these problems, the no hands up technique can be combined with thinking time to give more children a chance to participate.

It takes a while to get young children used to this technique, especially because so much effort will have already gone into getting them to sit still, listen and not call out. A visual cue will help, for example, a stick with a hand on it. When the practitioner points the hand upward it means 'this is a hands-up question' and when pointed down it means 'this is a hands-down question'. Also, children can be encouraged to use a different signal when they are ready to answer, such as crossed arms and a smile at the practitioner. This is less obvious for those children still thinking.

Clarke (2005) explains that this technique helps to increase focus because the children know they need to listen and think of an answer, as there is always a chance that they could be picked. It is possible, however, that some children will not respond well to being put under this type of pressure and begin to dread being chosen. This is why it is so important to spend a lot of time creating a positive learning culture as explained on page 25. Practitioners can also:

- Plan and differentiate their questions carefully so that all children will be able to answer something at some point.

- Use their knowledge of the children's individual abilities to pick particular children to answer each question.

- Take care when responding to a wrong answer by not being dismissive and using the child's contribution as a positive learning opportunity.

Random selection

Clarke (2005) suggests using a random method of selection that takes the choice out of the teacher's hands. Surprisingly, rather than feeling threatened at the prospect of being picked, she found this to be more favourable with children because they knew the teacher was not making the choice. Ideas for this are:

- pick out of a hat

- spin the bottle

- computer generated loop.

These methods are probably more suitable for older children who might better cope with the pressure. If using these methods with younger children, it is best only to do so if they are confident with the subject matter. Otherwise it is possible to make the random selection before asking the question, so that the practitioner can ask a question that is aimed at the level of the individual child.

Talk partners

As briefly mentioned earlier, it is helpful to give children the opportunity to discuss their thoughts with a talk partner, buzz partner or talk buddy. As well as giving them time to think of an answer it gives children a chance to articulate and clarify their thoughts by explaining them to another person – an important part of the thinking process. For those children who are less confident it is a chance to practice their answer on a friend before sharing it with a larger group. Harrison and Howard (2009) explain there is also the benefit of safety in numbers because the answer is coming from a group rather than an individual, which may feel less threatening.

There are various options available for organising talk partners:

- According to friendship: Children might be more comfortable sharing their ideas with others from within their circle of friends. Organising talk partners in this way may be more beneficial to those children who lack confidence or speak English as an additional language (because they may prefer to talk in their mother tongue).

- Mixed ability: Arranging children into mixed ability pairs is helpful because those who are less able have the opportunity to learn from another, and those who are more able consolidate their own understanding by explaining it to someone else.

- Random draw: Names can be picked out of a hat at the beginning of each half term, or more frequently on a weekly or fortnightly basis. Once paired the children are talk partners until the next draw. This random pairing is good for developing personal and social skills because children will inevitably be required to work with someone they might not usually play with. Being paired in such a way will also result in children being exposed to a variety of perspectives and points of view (Clarke, 2005).

Posing a question to a group of four-year-olds, telling them to discuss it for two minutes and come up with an answer is a challenge of the tallest order. Young children will need help and guidance in making the most effective use of their paired discussion time. This will involve some training.

Tips for training talk partners

- Concentrate on the basics: Teach the children about good talking and good listening. Ask them to help to identify features of good talking and listening. Produce a pictorial guide to refer to, featuring captioned photographs of the children. For example: A good talking guide could have three photographs captioned, 'look at your partner', 'speak clearly' and 'be kind even if you do not agree'. A good listening guide could feature three photographs captioned, 'look at your partner', 'try to sit still' and 'wait until they have finished before replying'.

- Provide an example: Pair up with a teaching assistant and show the children how it is done. Conversely, it is also an idea to show them how it is *not* done. Getting the children to point out where it has gone wrong and asking them for suggestions about how to put it right is more beneficial because it requires active thought.

- Focus on the familiar: At the beginning pose simple questions that the children will answer easily. For example, at the start of the year it is most logical to focus on getting to know each other. Conversation is easier when children can draw from a familiar frame of reference and most children will be confident to talk about themselves.

- Get children to report back: Clarke (2005) suggests regularly getting children to relay what their partner has said. This aims to improve concentration and listening skills.

- Circulate and listen in: Help to keep children on task and focused on the subject by circulating and pausing to listen in on their conversations. Practitioners can also take the opportunity to intervene and prompt children who appear to be struggling.

- Share interesting conversations: Take notes of anything interesting that the children say when talking with their partner. When talking time is over, share these snippets with the rest of the group. This will have a motivational affect because children will be pleased if their thoughts are picked out for sharing.

'Having talk partners as a regular feature of lessons allows all children to think, to articulate and therefore extend their learning. Shy, less confident children have voice, and over-confident children have to learn to listen to others, so the benefits extend to a more respectful, cooperative ethos and culture.'

(Clarke, 2005, p.55)

Multiple-choice

Another way to elicit a response is to ask children multiple-choice questions. Clarke (2005) proposes a number of different ways that this can be done. She suggests that these techniques are best used with talk partners rather than in a whole-class situation. The techniques do lend themselves well to early years teaching because focused work tends to be done with small groups anyway. Her ideas are outlined below; some are simplified and all are considered with young children in mind:

- Supply a range of answers: Ask a question and give children some answers to consider. With very young children it is best to provide a right and wrong answer. The children are then required to explain why one answer is right and the other is wrong. With children who are a little older it might be possible to add a further 'maybe' or 'it depends' answer that triggers a debate. An example question might be, 'What is the best junk material to make a boat that floats?' The right answer could be 'a plastic tub', the wrong answer 'tissue paper', and the maybe/depends answer 'lollipop sticks'.

- Make a statement and ask if the children agree or disagree: This is a good strategy for helping practitioners find out how much the children understand about a subject because they are required to explain their reasons. It is also useful for getting children to think about and communicate their personal views and opinions. For example, 'Jack should never have taken the golden egg from the giant' or 'It is easier to carry water in a bucket than a watering can'.

- Use the opposite: Think of a question and re-word it so that the children are required to consider two opposing possible answers. Examples of such questions are, 'Why is this one a repeating pattern and this one not?' and 'Why is this sand castle still standing, while that one has collapsed?'

- Ask 'Why?': Give the children the answer to a question and ask them, 'Why?' For example, 'Blocks are great for building towers. Why?' or 'Fairy cakes are made with self-raising flour. Why?'

- Ask the children to consider a different point of view: Clarke points out that this is a very effective technique for developing personal, social and emotional skills – an area of development that is particularly important in the Foundation Stage and Key Stage 1. Questioning in this way is a good way of helping children to solve disputes and tackle issues that are part of everyday life in an early years setting. For example, 'How do you think he feels now that you have taken that from him?' or 'Why might the other children prefer that you wash your hands before you share the grapes?'

Survey the group

Another technique, which is useful during whole-class carpet time or when working with large groups, is to survey the children and discuss the result. For example:

- A show of hands: This is particularly useful when asking who agrees or disagrees. Ask the question, get a show of hands and then pick individual children to explain why. Where the split is relatively equal, children can be paired so that they can explain their opposing views.

- Pose – pause – pounce – bounce: This is sometimes known as gathering. Ask a question; give children time to think; choose someone to answer; then immediately choose another and continue to bounce and gather several answers. Record the answers without responding straight away, then return to them and discuss them at the end.

- Whiteboards: Get the children to write their answer down on a whiteboard and reveal after a count of three. All children have a chance to think about their answer and respond. This method also helps practitioners to quickly survey the whole group and gain an overview of how many children understand.

A question a day

Display a question near the entrance to the setting for the children to answer on arrival each day. Provide somewhere for children to write their responses (ask parents to help younger children). This might be a pile of paper with a post box, a flip pad on an easel or a large whiteboard. Questions might include, 'What is your favourite cereal and why?' or 'Would you prefer a vegetable or flower patch outside? Why?'

> ### More information
>
> Find more ideas and information about how to build children's confidence and encourage them to participate in the following books:
>
> - *Helping Young Children Speak with Confidence* by Ros Bayley, Lynn Broadbent and Andrina Flinders (Lawrence Educational Publications).
>
> - *Communication, Language and Literacy from Birth to Five* by Avril Brock and Carolynn Rankin (Sage).

Encouraging children to work in a group

The following are ideas for group activities that require children to share information and enter into discussion. The activities are commonly used with older children further up the school, however it is possible to use them with younger children in reception and Key Stage 1. Most involve children moving around the classroom and so take a lot of practice, patience and support at the beginning. It is important to remember that at this early stage, doing these activities is more about getting children used to working in this way rather than the quality of the discussion. At this point practitioners are helping children to develop the skills they need to be able to cope with such activities.

Snowballing

This is sometimes referred to as think-pair-share. Children are asked to consider a question and discuss it with a partner. Each pair then joins with another pair to make a group of four and they share their ideas. Each group then joins with another group to make eight and they share their ideas again.

Jigsaw

The children are divided into groups of four and asked to find out about a particular aspect of something. Taking a food theme, for example:

- Younger children are divided into groups and given a piece of fruit to examine. The children are asked to taste their fruit, feel it and look at its features.

- Older children are given a piece of fruit and some simple information books about it. They are asked to taste and examine the fruit and find out something about it, such as how and where it is grown.

After an appropriate length of time the groups stop and each child in each group is given a number – one, two, three and four. They are then asked to split and form new number groups – all the ones, twos, threes and fours join together. The children then tell the others in their new group what they found out about their particular piece of fruit.

Carousel

The success of this activity depends upon the number of practitioners available. Therefore, it is best to do this when there are plenty of adults around, such as classroom assistants, students or parent helpers. Each adult is provided with a different coloured marker and a large piece of paper. The children are divided up and allocated to an adult. Each group considers the same question. Children offer their ideas and comments and these are recorded on the sheet of paper by the practitioner.

The sheets of paper are then rotated around the room to the next group. The practitioner reads out the other group's comments and asks the children for their response. The practitioner then records these views and responses on the same sheet in the different-coloured pen. The sheets continue to be rotated until they arrive back with their original groups. The structure and control that this activity offers really helps practitioners to get young children thinking about and responding to each other's ideas.

Tips for supporting group discussion

- With the youngest children it is best to spend time getting them used to working in groups before attempting any of the above activities. Stick to groups of four or six and place them with an adult.

- Younger children will need help to remain focused and take turns when speaking in their group. Help with this by organising them into a circle and giving them an object for the speaker to hold and pass on when they are finished.

- Guide the children in their discussion. Ask a question and take their responses one at a time. Help them to think about what each other has said by interjecting and asking for their views and opinions about what has been said.

- Older children will be able to work in groups more independently. This makes it possible to pose a question to a whole class and ask them to consider it in groups. Circulate around the room, observe and listen in to the groups' discussions. Look out for the children who are most and least confident. Think about who dominates the conversation and who tends to just listen or switch off. Gathering this information is helpful for dividing children into better-balanced groups in the future and deciding where it is best to place support assistants.

- Join the group. Listen and pick out interesting points the children make: Ask questions and encourage them to elaborate; ask for the other children's views and opinions about what is being said.

- Listen in and record interesting comments and ideas, and raise these for discussion with the rest of the class later.

A puppet assistant

Vicki Charlesworth (2005) recommends using a puppet to watch over the children as they work. This puppet can then feed back to everyone (practitioner included) at the end of the activity. This helps children to focus and stay on task. It also helps to boost self-esteem because the children are so pleased to have their efforts noticed.

Puppet pictures

Puppets can also be used to extend and sustain shared thinking. Ros Bayley (2006) suggests setting up photographs of puppets and soft toys doing interesting things and presenting them to the children for contemplation. This is an exceptionally engaging technique that instantly grabs the children's attention and draws them into discussion. The puppets can be placed in precarious or interesting situations to provoke discussion and debate that extends and deepens children's thinking. This is especially true if the pictures feature characters from the children's setting. Some ideas include:

- Photograph puppets doing dangerous or risky activities: Show pictures of puppets climbing on walls, running into the road, swinging on gates or jumping off rocks. Ask the children to talk about what the puppets are doing, predict what could happen and consider the consequences.

- Use puppets to create rules and responsibilities for the setting: Photograph them doing things like running in the classroom, snatching toys or fighting. Present these pictures to the children and ask them to consider the consequences of the puppets' actions. Ask the children to help devise a code of conduct in light of this discussion.

- Use puppets to get children thinking about everyday routines and activities: Take photographs of puppets doing the shopping, riding on a bus, going to the library, using the post office, cooking up a recipe or eating out somewhere. Show sequences of photographs and ask the children to talk about what is happening. Otherwise show isolated photographs and ask the children to consider what happens next, drawing from their own personal experiences. Photographs can also be shown out of sequence for the children to order themselves.

More ideas

Find more ideas about how to help extend and sustain shared thinking in these books:

- *Storylines: An Anthology of 50 Ideas For Using Large Puppets, Dolls and Soft Toys in Early Years Settings* by Ros Bayley and Lynn Broadbent (Lawrence Educational Publications).

- *Sustaining Shared Thinking* by Jenni Clarke (A&C Black).

- *Supporting Young Children's Sustained Shared Thinking* by Marion Dowling (The British Association of Early Childhood Education).

Helping children to question

Once children are beginning to respond and are picking up the skills they need to think about and answer questions, practitioners can build on this by teaching them how to question in order to further their own knowledge. Teaching children questioning skills is a step towards helping them to become independent learners. If children are able to question for themselves they will need less guidance from practitioners and become more adept at leading their own learning. Following are some suggestions for helping children to develop their questioning skills:

Join children's play

Potter (2008) suggests practitioners join children's play and talk about what they are doing. The aim of this is to make the children curious and encourage them to ask the practitioner questions about what they are doing.

Show and ask

Instead of bringing children to the front to show and tell, ask them to show and encourage everyone else to ask questions.

Games

- Who am I?: Take on the persona of a well-known children's storybook or television character and invite the children to ask questions to find out who it is.

- Guess who?: Play Guess Who? (by Hasbro, available from various toy shops and online). This game encourages children to ask questions about appearance to guess the identity of the other player's chosen character.

- Guess the hidden object: Hide an object in a feely bag and get the children to ask questions that help them to narrow down what it is.

Hot seating

Either a practitioner or child takes on the role of a character and fields questions from the group. This is a good drama activity for linking with a current story or theme. For example, the wolf from Little Red Riding Hood might be arrested and put in the dock for questioning; or an astronaut might be taking questions from the press about his recent expedition to the moon.

Interview visitors

Invite a visitor into the setting. Before the visit sit down with the children and ask them what they would like to find out. Help the children to formulate questions that will help them to gain this information. On the day of the visit rehearse the questioning with the children to help them prepare.

When, where, who, how and why cards

Harrison and Howard (2009) describe this method used by a Year 2 teacher. Children are given individual cards that read when, where, who, how and why. At certain points the teacher pauses and asks the children to think of a question that will help move the lesson on. For example, during a science lesson about growing, the teacher might show the children pictures of a live and dead plant. He may then challenge those children holding why, what or how cards to ask a question. The other children in the class can then offer their opinion about how good the questions are, offer suggestions for alternative questions, and also attempt the answer.

More ideas

Find more ideas about how to encourage children to question and develop enquiring minds in these books:

- *Helping Young Children to Ask Questions by Vicki Charlesworth (Lawrence Educational Publications).*

- *But Why?: Developing Philosophical Thinking in the Classroom by Sara Stanley, published by (Network Continuum Education).*

Planning AfL

This section looks at the planning that supports Assessment for Learning. It explains the importance of involving the children in the planning process and suggests ideas for activities that provide the best opportunities for formative assessment. There is also advice about how to plan for assessment and ensure that it is used to inform future teaching.

Planning with the children

'Central to assessment for learning is empowering learners through developing learning autonomy. This means involving learners in their own learning not just through reflection but also as co-constructors and co-negotiators of their learning.'

(Spendlove, 2009, p.x)

AfL practice means involving children from the outset. Planning should be done with the children to help get an idea of their current knowledge and understanding, and to find out what their particular interests might be. This ensures that activities, projects or tasks are planned to start at the right level and will help to further learning.

Involving children in planning gets them thinking about their learning by identifying what they do not yet know and what they need to learn. Children also decide what they would like to find out about, which increases their interest and motivation. Practitioners bring children back to the planning, ask them what they have learned and show them their progress, which also has a motivational effect. Following are a number of suggestions for involving children in the planning process.

Mind-mapping

At the beginning of a topic bring the children together and ask them what they already know. Create a mind-map – a spider-gram or topic web – of their current knowledge. This will also help to reveal any misconceptions that the children might have. Ask them what they would like to know about the topic. Record their questions and ideas in another colour on the same mind-map. Display the mind-map in an area that is easily accessible so that ideas can be altered or added. Use the mind-map as a basis for planning.

KWL grid

Harrison and Howard (2009) describe a method that involves recording what children 'Know' and 'Want to know' about a topic on a grid that also has a third column for eventually recording what the children have 'Learnt'. Display the grid in an area that is in clear view of children, practitioners and parents and return to it periodically during the topic to review it with the children. Ask the children to help update the 'Learnt' column by telling the practitioner what they now know.

Keyword cards

This method, also suggested by Harrison and Howard (2009), is more suited for use with small groups. The group is given a set of keyword cards about a topic. Children are then asked to pick a card, share it with the group and share some information they know about the word. Other children are then invited to add more information or comment on what someone else has said. This activity enables the practitioner to gain a good idea about how much the children know about various aspects of a topic, as well as which areas seem to enthuse the children the most.

Question tree (method one)

Introduce the topic to the children and ask them to go home and think about what they would like to learn about it. Send a note home to explain this to parents. Mount a picture of a leafless tree in the cloak area, or somewhere that is easily accessible to parents, and provide some green sticky notes and pens. On return to the setting, ask children and parents to record their questions on the notes and stick them to the tree branches. Use these questions as starting points for planning.

Question tree (method two)

Mount a picture of a leafless tree somewhere in plain view to adults and children. Ask the children what they already know about a topic and record their comments around the tree roots. Ask the children for any questions they might have and list these on the trunk. At the conclusion of the topic ask the children to feed back what they have learned. Record their comments on leaves and stick them to the tree branches (a pictorial representation of their knowledge growing).

Learning wall

Allocate a low-level wall display or section of wall space for this. Mark out 'ground level', leaving space underneath for the wall's 'foundations'. Record what the children already know about a topic in the underground space – the foundations upon which they are going to build their knowledge. Ask the children for any questions they might have or if there is anything in particular that they would like to find out about the topic. Record these comments and questions at ground level. Keep a supply of brick-shaped paper for recording new learning. Gather the children at regular intervals during the topic and record any new learning on the bricks. Stick the bricks on the display to build a wall. This is a great visual way of demonstrating to the children how their knowledge is growing.

Planning activities that support AfL

Once it has been established what the children know, want to know and need to learn, practitioners can then begin to plan how the children are going to learn about it. Collaborative activities designed to make children share their thoughts, and demonstrate their knowledge, understanding and skills, support AfL because they enable practitioners to discover how much the children understand. Practitioners can then build on this to develop and extend their thinking further. Activities that promote conversation and discussion include:

Challenges

Pose a challenge and get the children to tackle it together. Challenges might be curriculum related, such as building a bridge that will withstand the weight of a child or creating a menu for the role-play cafe. Otherwise they might be linked to setting issues, for instance, thinking of a solution to neighbourhood cats digging up the vegetable garden or painting aprons repeatedly getting trampled on and torn. Children can be invited to share ideas, plan a solution and carry it out.

Projects

Plan small and large-scale projects around something of particular interest to the children. This could be anything from superheroes to potatoes. Ask the children what they would like to find out and use their ideas as a starting point for planning various group activities that explore different aspects of the topic. Projects are fantastic for enthusing children and getting them talking.

Investigations

Set up in-depth group investigations that get children talking about what they can see, as well as about what and why things are happening. For example: helping to make play dough and experimenting with added extras like sand or glitter; attempting to freeze different substances like paint, fruit juice or slime; or creating different effects using a light box and coloured resources. Display questions around the investigation area for adults to pose to the children in order to trigger discussion.

Group excursions and explorations

When out and about, plan in some time for children to pause and explore properly. For example, while at a beach or on a park visit, group children with adults and send them on scavenger hunts or nature trails. Instruct the adult to gather the children at various points where there is an opportunity to explore something interesting, for instance, a rock pool, dead uprooted tree or patch of wild flowers. Equip the children with magnifiers, containers to collect things in and digital cameras. Activities like this provide a rich arena for children to share their thoughts and reveal their current understandings.

More ideas

Find plenty of ideas for collaborative group activities in the following books:

- *The Little Book of Explorations* and *The Little Book of Investigations* by Sally Featherstone (A&C Black).

- *Critical Skills in the Early Years* by Vicki Charlesworth, published by (Network Continuum Education).

Learning objectives and success criteria

Assessment that promotes learning 'involves sharing learning goals' with learners and helps learners 'to know and to recognise the standards they are aiming for' (ARG, 1999, p.7). This means ensuring learning objectives are clearly communicated to the children, and that they understand the criteria they need to meet in order to achieve these objectives.

WALT and WILF

Many practitioners, especially Key Stage 1 teachers, will be familiar with WALT and WILF. Often depicted as cartoon characters holding up signposts, they are used to communicate learning objectives and success criteria to the children. The two anagrams stand for: We Are Learning To… and What I am Looking For is…

When planning:

- Try not to identify too many success criteria. Stick to a maximum of three for each task, and even less for very young children.

- Make the learning objectives child friendly and think about providing examples to support success criteria.

The importance of clearly communicating learning objectives and success criteria to children is explored in more detail in the following section about feedback and assessment.

Helpful, flexible and formative planning

It is important to design any planning so that it includes information that supports the practitioner in their practice of AfL. Planning should detail:

- Learning objectives and success criteria in child-friendly language – or include space for this to be added once decided with the children.

- Ideas for questions and key vocabulary that will help to facilitate discussion.

- Assessment methods, including self and peer-assessment.

- How feedback will be given.

- Space for recording observation and assessment notes.

- Space for recording future implications of this assessment.

The example on the next page, taken from a reception teacher's planning for a topic on minibeasts, illustrates how this looks in practice. This adult-initiated focused activity was carried out with groups of four children at a time throughout the course of a week.

Reception – Summer 1 – Week 3 – 20/06/08   Minibeasts

Activity

Close examination and investigation of the minibeast habitat in the outdoor area.

Assessment methods

Observation

Questioning

Verbal feedback during discussion

Learning Objectives

We are learning to:

…look closely at something to find out more about it. (KUW)

…describe what something looks like and how it moves. (KUW)

…answer questions why. (KUW)

Success Criteria

What I am looking for:

The use of magnifiers to look closely.

Good describing words.

Trying hard to think of ideas about why.

Questions

Do you know what that is?

Why do you think it is doing that?

Why do you think they like to live there?

What is the difference between this insect and that one?

Is there any way we can make this habitat better for the insects?

Why do you think there are no… here?

Vocabulary

bark, soil, damp, warm, cold, sunny, wet, rainy, insect, moist, hidden, sheltered, dry, food, legs, crawl, climb, slime, slither, creepy, quick, slow

Observations

Children could name other minibeasts that were not there but were unable to think of where they might be found.

Implications for future planning
(next steps)

Minibeast hunt.

'Effective planning for young children's experiences becomes derailed if pre-written learning objectives or intentions are treated as inflexible.'

(Lindon, 2011, p.17)

It is also a good idea to make planning flexible to accommodate changes based upon on-going assessment. Planning should not be set in stone and practitioners should not be afraid to change their plans as a session or topic progresses. A planning file owned by an AfL practitioner will be covered in notes and alterations. Furthermore, it is important to ensure that children are given the time and opportunity to act on feedback and improve their work.

Teachers developing AfL practice in Jersey ensured flexibility by planning activities for Monday to Wednesday, leaving Thursday and Friday free. The idea was to spend Thursday reflecting upon the week with the children and identifying those areas that needed revisiting or extending. Friday would then be spent doing just that. Otherwise, Thursday would be used as a self or peer-assessment day, when children assessed the work produced earlier in the week. Friday's lesson would then be spent revisiting the work to act on the assessment and feedback.

The following pages show examples of a weekly literacy plan from a Year 1 teacher shows how this looks in practice. The planner details lessons for Monday to Wednesday, leaving Thursday free to review the week so far. During the Thursday session, practitioners work with small groups to assess their understanding. They then plan Friday's lesson to address any areas that need revisiting and consolidating. Suggestions for the use of AfL techniques are included, as well as ideas for questions. Space is also provided for handwritten assessment notes. (The example is transferable to Foundation Stage teaching.)

> ## More information
>
> The book below is an excellent resource. It provides detailed guidance and examples of planning AfL from Foundation Stage through to secondary level:
>
> * *Active Learning through Formative Assessment* by Shirley Clarke (Hodder Education).

Literacy – Books by Julia Donaldson

Monday

Learning Objectives	Success Criteria	Assessment
We are learning to...	**What I am looking for is...**	**Methods:**
Read a story out loud and make it sound interesting (T1)	Pausing at commas	Observation, questioning and peer-assessment
Look out for full stops, commas and speech marks (S1)	Stopping at full stops	
	Interesting voices for characters	
	Ideas for story endings	**Notes:**
Think about what happens next (En2,3b)	Reasons why you like different ideas	Some great ideas for what might happen next.
Talk about what we like and why (En2,3c)		

Introduction			Group Work	Questions
Text level	**Word/Sentence level**	**L**	**With teacher** Talk about might happen next. Choose an idea and act it out. Ask children to comment on each other's ideas. (Peer-assessment)	What do you think happens next? What would you like to happen next? Why do you think that character would do that? Which ideas do you like best? Why? Is there anything you want to change? What do you think about what actually happened?
Start reading *Room on the Broom*. Stop on page ? Ask children to predict what is going to happen next. (Snowballing)	Focus on reading with expression – taking account of full stops, commas, voices etc.	**M**	**With TA** Talk about might happen next. Choose an idea and act it out. Ask children to comment on each other's ideas. (Peer-assessment)	
				Plenary
		H	**Independently** Work together to make up an idea and act it out.	Find out what actually happened next. Compare children's ideas with the actual story. Ask children to comment on each other's ideas. (Peer-assessment)

Learning Objectives	Success Criteria	Assessment
We are learning to… Understand how stories are put together (T1) Use the past tense when retelling a story (S3) Retell a story (En2, 3b)	**What I am looking for is…** Story events in the right order Knowing what happens next Using the past tense	**Methods:** Observation, questioning and self-assessment **Notes:** *Most children able to sequence events. LA struggled a bit with identifying most significant parts. Needed quite a bit of guidance.*

Introduction			Group Work	Questions
Text level	**Word/Sentence level**	**L**	**With TA** Discuss which were most significant parts of story. (Talk partners) Create storyboard and check against book. (Self-assessment)	Can you tell me what happened in the story? Who were the main characters? What were the most important bits of the story? What happened next? How can we check you are right?
Start reading *Room on the Broom*. Stop on page ? Ask children to predict what is going to happen next. (Snowballing)	Focus on reading with expression – taking account of full stops, commas, voices etc.	**M**	**Independently** Create storyboard (sequencing cards to help) Check against the book (Self-assessment)	
				Plenary
		H	**With teacher** Discuss which were most significant parts of story. (Talk Partners) Create storyboard check against book. (Self-assessment)	Sing Room on the Broom song – to consolidate sequence of story events.

Wednesday

Learning Objectives	Success Criteria	Assessment
We are learning to...	What I am looking for is...	**Methods:**
Notice the difference between spoken stories and storybooks (T3)	Describing what the book sounds like	Observation, questioning and peer-assessment
Use different words that mean the same thing (W10)	Describing what I sound like without the book	**Notes:**
Think about the difference between telling and reading stories (En2,3d)	Ideas for different words	Children found thinking of different words difficult – especially those working independently. Had to abandon and bring group together for more input. This needs more time spent.

Introduction			Group Work	Questions
Text level	**Word/Sentence level**	**L**	**With teacher** Children retell the story with extra description to a partner.	How does the book sound different? Can you think of any more words to describe...? Why is that a better word? What does that word make you think about the...? Which word do you think works best there?
Retell the story. Ask children to listen out for why it is different to the book. Discuss and feed back. (Talk Partners)	When retelling use different language and descriptive words. Create a word bank of descriptive words that mean the same to describe different events and characters.	**M**	**With TA** Children retell the story with extra description to their group. Help children improve on each other's descriptions. (Peer-assessment)	
				Plenary
		H	**Independently** Children retell the story with extra description to their group (pictures and props to help).	Talk about which is best – story told with or without book.

Revisit and Review

The class could retell the story together.

Children found yesterday's lesson difficult – need to spend more time on widening range of vocabulary.

Children said they enjoyed making up their own story ending.

Learning Objectives	Success Criteria	Assessment
We are learning to... Use different words that mean the same thing (W10) Make up a character to go with the story (EN2,3f)	**What I am looking for is...** An interesting character Plenty of describing words Words that mean the same thing	**Methods:** Observation, questioning and teacher assessment of work produced. **Notes:** This helped to consolidate understanding of words that mean the same. Children need to revisit this.

Introduction	Group Work		Questions
Explain that the children are to make up their own story character for Room on the Broom. Children to draw a picture and surround it with different words to describe their character. Aim to try and think of as many words as possible that mean the same thing. (Traffic light fans)	**L**	**With teacher** Create character together. Children suggest as many words as possible – teacher to scribe.	What does that word mean? Can you think of another word that means the same? Can you describe your character? What do you think of that character? What makes you think that?
	M	**With TA** Create character together. Children suggest and write words with help.	**Plenary**
	H	**With student** Create a character each. Use word bank created on Wednesday to help write words.	Show characters and ask rest of children in class to think of more words to describe them. (Pose – pause – pounce – bounce)

Assessment and feedback strategies

'The awareness of learning and ability of learners to direct it for themselves is of increasing importance in the context of encouraging lifelong learning.'

(ARG, 1999, p.8)

Black and Wiliam's review of the research found that a key factor in improving learning through assessment depends on learners being actively involved in their own learning by being 'able to assess themselves and understand how to improve' (ARG, 1999, p.5). This is supported by the Excellence and Enjoyment document, which explains that AfL is particularly important for meeting learners' individual needs because children are viewed as partners in their learning: self-assessing and setting personal targets (DfES, 2003). This section looks at a number of techniques that help young children to get actively involved in the assessment of their own learning.

Involving children in deciding success criteria

The previous section mentioned the importance of sharing learning goals and success criteria with the children. Children need to understand the purpose of the learning; what they are doing and why they are doing it. They also need to understand what good quality is, where they are in terms of achieving this and what they can to do to achieve it. If children understand what they are aiming for and what they need to do, they are more likely to succeed. It follows that if children are involved in thinking about and deciding what steps they need to take to reach a goal, they are more likely to stay focused and remember what they need to do. There are a number of ways that this can be done:

- Tell the children what the goal of the activity is and ask them what they need to do to achieve it. For example, the goal might be to create a repeating pattern. The children are asked to explain what a repeating pattern looks like and how they might create one using coloured threading beads and laces. The practitioner then uses this to formulate some success criteria: choose just two colours, check that every other bead is the same.

- Clarke (2005) provides examples of posters featuring success criteria for reading and writing. These posters, produced with the help of reception children, were displayed on the classroom walls as permanent reminders for the children to refer to and check what they needed to do.

- If creating photographic guides (as explained on page 56), it is a good idea to involve the children in taking the photographs and to ask them for suggestions for captions. The children's involvement and collaboration in creating the guides and identifying success criteria makes them more memorable and effective.

'… successful learning occurs when learners have ownership over their learning; when they understand the goals they are aiming for; when crucially, they are motivated and have the skills to achieve success.'

(ARG, 1999, p.2)

Helping children to communicate their understanding

Being able to self-assess is important because it enables children to keep the practitioner informed about their level of understanding. If children can communicate to the practitioner how far they understand something the practitioner can adjust their teaching to address any difficulties the children might be having. Following are some techniques that children can use to communicate their understanding to practitioners:

Thumb tool

As well as helping children to communicate their understanding, this tool can also be used to help children to convey their thoughts and opinions about something. If they fully understand or are in agreement about something they hold their thumb up. If they do not understand or are in disagreement they hold their thumbs down. If they are undecided or unsure they hold up a closed fist. An alternative to this is the use of a fan with segments featuring a smiley face ☺, sad face ☹, or expressionless face ☺.

Traffic lights

In this case, green means the children fully understand, red means they do not and amber means they are unsure. There are a number of ways that the traffic light tool can be used:

- Self-assessment during whole-class or group teaching: Children are given a fan with red, green and yellow segments. When asked if they understand something, they hold up the applicable colour. This is a good way of helping the practitioner gain an overview of how many children understand.

- Self-assessment during a group activity: Older children can be given a set of three coloured cards. During whole-class desk-based learning they can place a card in front of them to indicate how well they understand and are progressing with the activity. The teacher can then zone in on and help those showing red and amber cards. Another idea is to pair up children showing green and amber cards, to enable the teacher to focus on the red (Clarke, 2005).

Helping children to assess themselves against success criteria

'…self-assessment by pupils, far from being a luxury, is in fact an essential component of formative assessment.'

(Black and Wiliam, 2001, p.7)

Teaching children how to assess their own and other's work helps them to understand what they are trying to achieve. Children learn how to check their work against success criteria, evaluate what they have done so far and think about the next steps they need to take to improve. Harrison and Howard describe this as teaching children to think about their thinking. This means being able to 'oversee and steer their own learning in the right direction so that they can take responsibility for it' (2009, p.6). Following are some ideas for helping young children become independent learners, who are able to assess themselves against success criteria.

Using photographs

The use of photographs is a particularly effective means of helping young children to assess themselves against success criteria. In the early years, much teaching is focused on personal and social skills, helping children to care for the classroom environment and develop independence. It is possible to use photographs to help remind children what they need to do in order to develop these skills. For example:

- Take photographs of areas around the setting when they are clean and tidy and display them in the corresponding areas. Point these out to the children when they are dropping their coats on the floor instead of hanging them on hooks, or putting jigsaw pieces into the nearest basket instead of in the correct box.

- Display photographs to help remind children how to look after themselves. For example, take photographs of children using soap to wash their hands, putting paper towels in the bin and flushing the toilet. Stick these photos next to the soap and paper towel dispensers and the toilet to jog the children's memory.

- Create visual instructions for children to check themselves against. Like the good speaking and listening guides mentioned earlier in the book, create guides to good sitting and lining up, for example. Refer to these as examples when asking children to do things.

Traffic lights

As well as helping children to communicate their understanding to adults, getting young children familiar with the use of the traffic light tool is helpful preparation for assessment methods used further up the school. Teachers in Key Stage 2 and above may use traffic light marking to assess written work. This involves the use of green and yellow highlighter pens to identify areas that meet success criteria and areas that need improvement. The same technique is also used by children assessing their own work as well as for peer-assessment. Young children can begin to learn how to do this too:

- Self-assessment of work produced: This requires a lot of guidance and support and will need to be done on a one-to-one basis with a practitioner. Children can either use coloured sticky dots or coloured pens or pencils. They are helped to check their piece of work against the success criteria. Before deciding to allocate themselves a green, red or amber spot to indicate how far they have achieved the objective. Whatever colour the child selects, the practitioner asks them to explain why and helps them to think about the next steps they need to take to improve.

Practitioner guidance

Practitioners can guide older children, who are working more independently, to begin checking themselves against success criteria while they work. This can be done in the following ways:

- Periodically remind children of the success criteria throughout an activity. This is especially important when working with younger children.

- Help children to check on their own progress by stopping them and asking them how they are doing. Check their understanding of the task and ask them what they are doing to achieve it. This helps to keep the children on track and focused on their goal.

- Offer comments and suggestions that help children act and improve. For example: 'Your drawing is very detailed. You now need to choose the right colours for it.' 'Tell me what you need to do next.' 'Have a look at the example. Is there anything you have missed?' Harrison and Howard (2009) offer many more suggestions for this.

'Even very young children have been found to be capable of thinking about how they feel about their learning and, over a longer period of time, they become more able to reflect upon the learning in relation to the agreed criteria.'

(Harrison and Howard, 2009, pp.6-7)

The formative use of observation evidence

'Any assessment you make should give you useful information, which contributes to the picture of the child that you are gradually building up. However, if you don't use the information you have collected, you are wasting time collecting it!'

(Featherstone, 2011, p.27)

Of course, formative assessment in the early years mostly involves observing children while they are engaged in child-initiated play. The purpose of gathering observations is to build a picture of a child's learning and use this information to plan experiences that will move them on further. It is possible to design observation records so that the relationship between this assessment and future planning is made more explicit. This involves allocating space for the practitioner to record assessment notes as well as implications for future planning.

It is possible to involve the children in this process. Practitioners can talk to children while they are observing them and ask them questions, much in the same way that they would during an adult-led activity. Observation notes can also be shared with the children and used as a basis for further questioning and discussion. Space can be allocated on the observation record for keeping a note of the children's comments. The following is an example of how this looks in practice:

KEY ISSUES: Assesment for Learning in the EYFS

Focused observation sheet

Child's name: Charlotte	Context: Free-flow play Play dough	Date: 04/05/2011
Age: 3 years		Start time: 10.13am
Observer: Melanie	Area of learning: PD, KUW	End time: 10.20am

Observation notes:

Charlotte picks up cutting wheel in right hand and rolls it at a chunk of play dough. The dough moves but cutter doesn't go over it. Charlotte presses the dough down with left hand and rolls cutter at it again. Cutter bumps into dough and dents it. Charlotte squashes dough down so it is flatter on table. Rolls cutter at it again. Cutter rolls over dough and leaves a mark. Charlotte rolls cutter quickly back and forward until dough is striped with cuts.

Charlotte peels dough off table and rolls it together in hands. Keeps squashing and squeezing for a while, and moulds into a ball. Presses ball onto table and bangs with right fist to flatten. Pats with right hand until flat. Picks up cutter again and rolls over and over to make stripy pattern again.

Discussion/Reflection with child:

When asked what she was doing Charlotte said she was 'cutting'. She said she couldn't get the cutter to work. When asked what she might do about it she picked dough off table and started again. She didn't do much different. When asked why the cutter wouldn't work she shrugged and said 'don't know'.

Assessment notes:

The dough was too thick for the cutter. Charlotte hasn't yet figured out that she needs to flatten it more. Didn't use the rolling pins.

Implications for future planning/Next steps:

Introduce Charlotte to some different malleable materials — salt dough, clay, etc.
Help Charlotte use different strategies to flatten dough — rolling pins etc.
Provide a variety of cutting and mark-making tools for her to experiment with.

Possible questions for investigation: Which dough is the easiest to cut/flatten? Which tools are best for cutting/ flattening each kind of dough?

Observation evidence is very useful for helping children to reflect upon their learning, especially photographic observations and digital video recordings, which 'provide a visual stimulus for discussion' (Sargent, 2011, p.27). As soon as possible after the activity the children can be brought to the photographs or video recording to reflect upon their activity. Practitioners can help with this by asking them to describe what they are doing, listening to their explanations, ideas and reasoning, and questioning to extend their thinking. The following are some ideas for questions that practitioners can ask:

- Can you tell me what you are doing?

- Why did you decide to do that?

- What is that you are using?

- Did you find it difficult doing that?

- What do you think you could have done to make it easier?

- Who is that with you?

- Are you working/ playing together?

- What are they doing?

- Why do you like to have them work/play with you?

- Can you tell me what happened?

- What did you find out about…?

- Are you happy with how that went?

- What would you do next time?

- Why do you think that?

When watching a video recording, play it through without sound at first to give the child a chance to talk about what they did without getting distracted. Then play it through a second time with sound so the child can comment on anything interesting that is said. Just like when using 'wait time', press pause at places where something interesting happens or when asking a question, to give the child time to think before commenting.

More information

Find examples of shared reflection between practitioners and children, as well as examples of observation documents that encourage formative use of information collected in the following book:

- *The Project Approach in Early Years Provision* by Marianne Sargent (Practical Pre-School Books).

Constructive feedback

'Assessment that promotes learning "provides feedback which leads to pupils recognising their next steps and how to take them"'

(ARG, 1999, p.7)

Black and Wiliam's review of the research found that a key factor in improving learning through assessment depends on the effective provision of feedback to learners (ARG, 1999). AfL practice involves bolstering children's confidence by highlighting areas of success, while helping them to improve by offering constructive and useful feedback. The following technique is especially effective in terms of offering children the information they need to be able to further their learning:

Two stars and a wish

This idea originates with the ARG and is widely used in Key Stage 2 and above, for teacher assessment as well as self and peer-assessment. However, it is just as effective with younger children, especially because it lends itself well to communicating assessment information visually. The idea is to offer two positive pieces of feedback (the stars) and identify one area for improvement (the wish).

When working with younger children it is a good idea to set up a display featuring two laminated stars that are large enough to write on or stick a picture inside. Alongside this display another shooting star (other ideas include a rocket or candle) to represent the wish. This display can be used as an aid to teaching very young children how to self-assess whole group tasks or challenges. For example, a practitioner might ask a group of children to assess how well they did at tidying up at the end of a session. He might give the children a camera and ask them to take a photo of two areas that look particularly neat and another that could do with a bit more effort. The pictures can be stuck to the display.

Alternatively, the children might be brought together to assess a large-scale roadway designed and built by a group of children during child-initiated play. The practitioner might ask the children comment on the areas that they feel have been well designed and offer a suggestion for how to develop and improve it. These comments can then be written on the stars and wish display.

As the children get used to this process they can begin to use the same method for individual peer-assessment. A child is invited to present a piece of work or something they have created to the group. Children are then asked to offer some positive comments about it – two stars – and one area for improvement – a wish. Charlesworth offers some advice with respect to this. She highlights the difficulty in getting young children to offer detailed descriptive comments about the work, pointing out the need for help with this. She also suggests that the child showing the work is allowed to choose who assesses it.

'This is important: it is their work and they should have control over who comments on it.'

(2005, p.71)

Conclusion

Perhaps the greatest advantage to introducing AfL practice to young children is that it helps them to develop the skills that lead to independent learning. The aim of this book has been to demonstrate that it is possible to involve even the youngest children in decision making about their own learning. Throughout, there have been suggestions for how to differentiate AfL strategies and techniques so that they can be used with children in the early years. It is hoped that by using this book, early years practitioners can start children on their journey towards becoming confident and independent life-long learners.

Bibliography

Assessment Reform Group (ARG) (1999) *Assessment for Learning: Beyond the Black Box*. Cambridge, University of Cambridge School of Education.

Assessment Reform Group (ARG) (2002) *Assessment for Learning: 10 Principles*. Institute of Education, University of London

Bayley R (2006) *Sustained Shared Thinking*. Training delivered in partnership with States of Jersey Education, Channel Islands.

Bayley R (2007) *Promoting Personal Social and Emotional Development*. Training delivered in partnership with Early Excellence, Huddersfield.

Black P and Wiliam D (2001) *Inside the Black Box: Raising standards through classroom assessment*. BERA Short. King's College London School of Education.

Bruce T (2005) *Early Childhood Education*. 3rd edn. London, Hodder Arnold

Call N (2005) *The Thinking Child*. Stafford, Network Educational Press

Charlesworth V (2005) *Critical Skills in the Early Years*. London, Network Continuum Education.

Clarke S (2005) *Formative Assessment in Action*. London, Hodder Murray.

Clarke S (2008) *Active Learning through Formative Assessment*. London, Hodder Education.

Council for the Curriculum, Examinations and Assessment (CCEA) (2006) *Northern Ireland Curriculum: Understanding the Foundation Stage*. Belfast, CCEA.

Department for Children, Education, Lifelong Learning and Skills (DCELLS) (2008) *Foundation Phase Framework for Children's Learning for 3 to 7-year-olds in Wales*. Cardiff, DCELLS Publications.

Department for Children, Schools and Families (DCSF) (2008a) *The Assessment for Learning Strategy*. Nottingham, DCSF Publications.

Department for Children, Schools and Families (DCSF) (2008b) *The Early Years Foundation Stage: Principles into Practice Cards*. Nottingham, DCSF Publications.

Department for Children, Schools and Families (DCSF) (2008c) *Standards Site: The National Strategies (Archived)*. Primary Strategy: Assessment for learning. Available from: http://webarchive.nationalarchives.gov.uk/20110202093118/http://nationalstrategies.standards.dcsf.gov.uk/primary/assessment/assessmentforlearningafl

Department for Education (DfE) (2011a) *Teachers' Standards*. London, The Stationery Office (TSO).

Department for Education (DfE) (2011b) *Statutory Framework for the Early Years Foundation Stage*. Draft for consultation, 6 July 2011. London, TSO. Available from: http://www.education.gov.uk/consultations/index.cfm?action=consultationDetails&consultationId=1747&external=no&menu=1

Department for Education and Skills (DfES) (2003) *Excellence and Enjoyment*. London, HMSO

Department for Education and Skills (DfES) (2005) *Every Child Matters Outcomes Framework*. London, HMSO.

Donaldson M (1978) *Children's Minds*. Glasgow, Fontana Press.

Featherstone S (2011) *Catching Them At It! Assessment in the early years*. London, A&C Black.

Harrison C and Howard S (2009) *Inside the Primary Black Box: Assessment for learning in primary and early years classrooms*. London, GL Assessment.

Katz L and Chard SC (2000) *Engaging Children's Minds: The Project Approach*. 2nd edn. USA, Ablex Publishing.

Learning and Teaching Scotland (LTS) (2011) *LTS: Learning, teaching and assessment*. Assessment as part of learning and teaching. Available from: http://www.ltscotland.org.uk/learningteachingandassessment/assessment/progressandachievement/howweassess/learningteachingandassessment/introduction.asp

Lindon J (2010) *Understanding Child Development*. 2nd edn. London, Hodder Education.

Lindon J (2011) *Planning for Effective Early Learning*. London, Practical Pre-School Books.

Marsden E, Woodbridge J, Drummond MJ (2005) *Looking Closely at Learning and Teaching*. Huddersfield, Early Excellence.

Moyles J, Adams S, Musgrove A (2002) *Study of Pedagogical Effectiveness in Early Learning*. Research Report No RR363. London, DfES Publications.

New Zealand Ministry of Education (1996) *Te Whāriki: Early Childhood Curriculum*. Wellington, Learning Media Limited.

Office for Standards in Education (Ofsted) (2008) *Assessment for learning: the impact of National Strategy support*. London, TSO.

Potter C (2008) 'Getting young children talking in early years settings.' In: Brock A and Rankin C (2008) *Communication, Language and Literacy from Birth to Five*. London, Sage.

Qualifications and Curriculum Development Agency (QCDA) (2011) *The National Curriculum Online*. Coventry, QCDA. Available from: http://curriculum.qcda.gov.uk/key-stages-1-and-2/index.aspx

Rinaldi C (2006) *In Dialogue with Reggio Emilia: Listening, researching and learning*. Oxon, Routledge.

Sargent M (2011 *The Project Approach in Early Years Provision*. London, Practical Pre-School Books.

Siraj-Blatchford I, Sylva K, Muttock S, Gilden R, Bell D (2002) *Researching Effective Pedagogy in the Early Years [REPEY]*. Research Report No 356. London, HMSO.

Siraj-Blatchford I, Sylva K, Melhuish E, Sammons P and Taggart B (2004) *Effective Provision of Preschool Education [EPPE]*: Final Report. Institute of Education, University of London.

Spendlove D (2009) *Putting Assessment for Learning into Practice*. London, Continuum International.

Tickell C (2011) *The Tickell Review: The Early Years: Foundations for life, health and learning*. London, TSO. Available from: http://www.education.gov.uk/tickellreview

UNICEF (2011) *A Better Life for Every Child: A Summary of the United Nations Convention on the Rights of the Child*. London, UNICEF. Available from: http://www.unicef.org.uk/Documents/Publications/rightsleaflet2011.pdf

Vygotsky L (1978) *The Mind in Society*. London, Harvard University Press.

Wiliam D (2009) *Assessment for Learning: Why, What and How?* Institute of Education, University of London.

Wood D, Bruner J and Ross G (1976) 'The role of tutoring in problem solving.' *Journal of Child Psychology and Psychiatry 17(2)*: 89-100.

Further reading

The following book offers a more theoretical perspective of the AfL principles. It outlines educational theory, highlights relevant research and looks at a variety of approaches to formative assessment:

Assessment for Learning in the Early Years Foundation Stage by Jonathan Glazzard, Denise Chadwick, Anne Webster and Julie Percival (Sage).

Also recommended

A Practical Guide to Child Observation and Assessment by Christine Hobart, Jill Frankel and Miranda Walker (Nelson Thornes)

Catching them at it by Sally Featherstone (A&C Black)

Like Bees not Butterflies: Child-initiated Learning in the Early Years edited by Sally Featherstone (A&C Black)

The Hundred Languages of Children: The Reggio Emilia Approach edited by Carolyn Edwards, Lella Gandini and George Forman (Ablex Publishing)

The Little Book of Parachute Play by Clare Beswick (A&C Black).

The Little Book of Playground Games by Simon MacDonald (A&C Black).

Unlocking Formative Assessment by Shirley Clarke (Hodder and Stoughton)